THE SIMPLE KEY TO
Great Presentations

How to create and deliver powerful presentations, even if you're not a great speaker

For Kelly, who is about to catch the next great big wave!

Larry [signature]

Larry Lansburgh

Copyright © 2014 Larry Lansburgh
All rights reserved.
ISBN: 1495464059
ISBN 13: 9781495464058

If you have a vision,
and need to speak that vision into the world,
this book is dedicated to you.

Table of Contents

Chapter 1
This Book 1

Chapter 2
The Simple Key to Great Presentations 7

Chapter 3
Have a Great Beginning 11

Chapter 4
Keep Them Close Together 31

Chapter 5
Have a great ending 47

Chapter 6
The Invitational Presentation 57

Chapter 7
Final Thoughts 79

Acknowledgements 89

CHAPTER 1

This Book

This book will show you how to create and deliver presentations that are far superior to most other people's—even if you're not a great speaker. All you need to do is follow the Simple Key to Great Presentations, which you will discover in the next chapter.

> **Presentation** (n) — A gathering that can have any or all of the following purposes:
> - invite its audience to do something
> - inform
> - inspire
> - entertain
>
> A presentation can include slides, video, and music in addition to the main speaker or speakers.

Whether the purpose of your presentation is to give a white paper to your State Assembly, protect an endangered species, or sell hydraulic actuators to an aerospace company, this book is for you. Whether you're in the non-profit or the for-profit world, you always need to connect with your audience. The Simple Key to Great Presentations will help you do just that.

What I call the Simple Key to Great Presentations revealed itself over the last several decades. As I created presentations—hundreds of live events, films, and videos—I always analyzed what had worked and what hadn't. When I watched other people's presentations, I noticed that the same techniques worked well, and the same mistakes always spoiled the event, even if the person standing in front of the audience was a good speaker.

The Simple Key to Great Presentations actually began to take form in my childhood. My father, Larry Lansburgh, Sr., was an Oscar-winning motion picture producer for Walt Disney. Pop transmitted some rock-solid principles of showmanship to my brother and me. "Boys," he said many times, "always leave your audience wanting more." I quote several of my father's gems of showmanship in this book.

How is this book different?

Google "how to give a presentation" and you'll get hundreds of millions of results. Go to Amazon.com, and you'll find more than 19,000 books on "how to be a speaker." I haven't had a chance to check out all of those millions of links or all 19,000 books, but I've followed up on quite a few. I discovered some good, common sense tips, but I never found what you will read in this book.

I'm surprised so few presenters apply the Simple Key to Great Presentations. I'm even more surprised that, to my knowledge, no one has written a book about it.

I've been using the Key for decades, and it works. It's my privilege to share it with you.

Why is this book is so slim?

This book is slim for several reasons. For one thing, it doesn't have any unnecessary filler or fluff. I see no connection between the thickness of a book and its importance.

Also, I haven't tried to cover every single aspect of speaking in front of a group. For example, your presentations will be better if you're a good speaker, but you can't learn those skills from a book. Chapter 7 tells you what you can do to become a good speaker.

In Chapter 4, I've written only a couple of hundred words on how to avoid PowerPoint abuse. That's the essence of it, but if you want to dig deeper into PowerPoint, you'll find hundreds of excellent articles and blogs on the internet.

Another reason this book is slim is that I refer to Steve Jobs only briefly. Granted, his presentations were masterful. They helped him not just to sell products, but also to create whole new markets and re-define entire industries. But I don't attempt to duplicate any of the excellent and detailed analyses of his presentations that already exist.

Finally, I haven't mentioned such crucial things as effective marketing for your event, how to overcome fear of public speaking, what you should wear, or your body language while you're in front of your audience.

This book concentrates on how you can use the Simple Key to Great Presentations to get superior results every time.

What you're about to read

For simplicity's sake, I've written this book as if you will be the only speaker. But maybe your event will feature several speakers. Maybe you're organizing the event, and you're not going to speak at all. Use this book as your guide whether your presentation involves speaking to five people in someone's living room, or to a thousand people in an auditorium.

If you understand your audience and apply the Simple Key to Great Presentations, you could stand in front of two thousand people and speak about the evolution of industrial adhesives in Eastern Europe in the 1970's, and your presentation would not be boring. It would be interesting.

It might even change someone's life.

Now check out the Key and how you can put it to use.

CHAPTER 2

The Simple Key to Great Presentations

It's simple, isn't it? And it is _the_ key.

> **Have a great beginning.**
> **Have a great ending.**
> **Keep them close together.**

Not a guideline

Don't think of the Key as a guideline. Think of it as a law. Break this law, and you will have a lousy presentation. Apply the law, and you will have a very good presentation.

Why is the Key effective?

The Key is so effective because it provides a structure, a framework that works for any kind of presentation.

"Structure." "Framework." These words may sound left-brained, cold, and overly rational, but they really aren't. The structure of your presentation supports a human relationship, the one you have with the people in your audience.

Every speaker has a different way of relating to an audience. Men and women often communicate differently. But the techniques you will discover in this book apply equally to everyone.

You may need to:
- give a briefing to your company's board of directors
- invite people to join your organization
- sell a product or service
- inspire people with the story of your comeback from a serious illness
- entertain your friends with a slide show of your trip to the Lake Country of England

No matter what your purpose, the Simple Key to Great Presentations shapes your relationship with your audience. This relationship determines your presentation's success or failure.

> *Never, ever bore your audience.*
> Larry Lansburgh, Sr. (1911 - 2001)
> Oscar-winning film producer

Does the Key really work?

Yes, it does. Over the years, I've seen mediocre speakers give excellent presentations because they had a great beginning, a great ending, and they didn't speak too long. I've also watched very good speakers do just the opposite, with the result that their event was boring, annoying, unfocused, and far too long.

Never, ever bore your audience.

Surprisingly, I have never found any link between people's expertise and their ability to deliver a good presentation. You might be the leading expert in your field, but if you don't follow the Key, you will have a presentation that could bore a toad.

What constitutes a great beginning? How do you create a great ending? How do you keep them close together? Keep reading.

CHAPTER 3

Have a Great Beginning

A great beginning starts in the very first minute of the planning stage, and it focuses entirely on the audience.

Most presenters (maybe even you) begin with what I call the "Me! Me! Me!" step. "Which PowerPoint slides will I use?" they say to themselves. "I think a Tuesday afternoon will work for me. What jokes should I use? Will I need to get a babysitter? I've gotta make sure I get all the right stuff into my briefcase."

Handle the "Me! Me! Me!" stuff later.

First, focus on your audience.

> *Everyone is in show business, but not everyone knows it.*
> Larry Lansburgh, Sr.

Your audience

The first step in planning your great beginning is to answer these questions:

1. Who is my audience?

    Be as specific as you can. "High school students interested in community activities" is far better than "Teenagers." If your presentation is for the general public, identify your ideal audience members. For example, "Men and women over 40 who are interested in nature."

2. How can I truly serve my audience?

    It's certainly enough to entertain or inform your audience and leave it at that. But if it's appropriate, are there further ways you can inspire and educate them? If, say, your presentation is about the wild birds of Alaska, are there bigger issues connected with those birds? Can you leave your audience with a new sense of the global importance of unspoiled nature?

3. What are their reasons for attending?

    Their reasons for attending might be different from how you think you can serve them. They might show up because they are in the neighborhood or because the event is free.

4. With all of the above in mind, what is a compelling title for the presentation?

    Your title will do one of two things. It will persuade people to stay away, or it will compel them to attend. Give your title a lot of thought. Brainstorm with other people. Most importantly, create a title that speaks to your audience. "My Alaska Slide Show" will keep people away. "Wild Birds of Alaska" at least says what it's about. "Little-Known Wild Birds of Alaska" is better. "Wild Birds of Alaska: What They're Telling Us about Drilling for Oil" is better still.

5. How long will this presentation be?

    The answer to this question has a strong impact on the third part of the Simple Key to Great Presentations. It's the first step you take to ensure that your beginning and your ending are close together. And it keeps you thinking about your audience. What is their attention span? Are they going to be relieved your speaking marathon has finally come to an end, or are you going to follow my father's advice and leave them wanting more?

    Most presentations shouldn't go more than an hour. You can usually accomplish everything you want to in even less time.

Use the following worksheet and refer to it often. You can download the identical worksheet free from my website (www.AmazonSpeaker.com).

My Audience

Who is my audience?

How can I truly serve my audience?

What are their reasons for attending?

With all of the above in mind, what is a compelling title for the presentation?

How long will this presentation be?

> *Begin, be bold, and venture to be wise.*
> Horace (65 BC - 8 BC)
> Soldier and lyric poet

One of my audiences

I was the keynote speaker for the California Student Sustainability Convergence, held on the Cal Poly campus in San Luis Obispo, California. The first thing I did was to find out as much as I could about my audience.

I learned that most people in my audience would be undergraduates from college campuses all over California. They and their organizations were deeply engaged in sustainability projects such as recycling programs, permaculture, more efficient technology, local agriculture, and bringing the concepts of sustainability to children. Many of them, I was sure, needed to persuade reluctant bureaucracies and non-cooperative corporations to embrace more sustainable activities. These were committed people. Every day their actions backed their passions. They were an impressive group, definitely people who had high standards and would not tolerate some mushy generalities from me. I had to give them something useful, something they could use on a day-to-day basis—and at the same time something interesting and entertaining.

I'd made a documentary film in the Amazon rain forest about an extraordinary group of indigenous people, the Achuar, who are successfully defending their territory from oil operations. I felt this rare indigenous success story would provide a good platform for the presentation. I was certain that if people in my audience had to come up against large, powerful organizations, they could use the same tactics the Achuar are using.

Here is how my worksheet looked.

My Audience

Who is my audience?
Undergraduates from college campuses around California. They are active in sustainability programs and projects.

How can I truly serve my audience?
I can provide them with specific tactics they can use in their sustainability efforts, especially if they are dealing with big, harmful organizations. On a larger scale, I can give them a global perspective on the importance of their actions. I can inspire them to keep going.

What are their reasons for attending?
Frankly, they're going to show up simply because my keynote address is the first event of the weekend. I assume that they hope the presentation will at least be interesting and at best be relevant to their interest in sustainability.

With all of the above in mind, what is a compelling title for the presentation?
> "David and Goliath in the Amazon:
> How a Small Indigenous Group
> Triumphed over Big Oil."

How long will this presentation be?
Forty-five minutes, plus fifteen minutes for questions and answers. One hour total.

Now it's time for your presentation.

You've used your worksheet to focus on your audience. You've done all the necessary preparation for the event. Now it's time for you to step in front of your audience. As people gather, everyone is going to be asking the same question. It is the same question you asked before every presentation you have ever attended. It is the same question you asked when you first picked up this book.

What's in this for me?

Sure, people in your audience have shown up because they know in general what your presentation is about. They expect to hear how your department's new developments in nano-technology will affect the bottom line. Or they know you will be speaking about indigenous people using computers. If it's a musical event, people are there because they're looking forward to an evening of ukulele music, a piano concerto by Rachmaninoff, or you singing grand opera.

> *The beginning is the most important part of the work.*
> Plato (428 - 348 BC)
> Philosopher and mathematician

But they will always ask themselves how they will benefit from the event. How you create and deliver the beginning is crucial because it sets the tone for the entire event. It answers the question *What's in this for me?*

The two elements of your great beginning:
- The introduction
- Your first words

Each element has its own specific purpose.

The introduction

Don't introduce yourself. Have someone else do it. The purpose of the introduction is to inform the audience of your expertise and why you are qualified to address the group.

But you need to create that introduction. Write it yourself, and give a hard copy in large print to the person who will introduce you. You might also want to insist that the person introducing you <u>not</u> say, "without further ado." This is a horrible cliché. Beside, "ado" means a fuss, especially about something unimportant. The introduction is a very important part of your presentation, and therefore is not "ado."

For my address as keynote speaker at the California Student Sustainability Convergence, I provided this introduction:

> Our speaker this morning is an Academy Award-nominated and Emmy-winning documentary filmmaker from Nevada City, California.
>
> His most recent film is a documentary about an extraordinary group of Amazonian indigenous people, who call themselves the Achuar. To make the film, our speaker traveled into the rain forest of southeastern Ecuador seven times. He conducted about fifty on-camera interviews and had some three hundred informal conversations with Achuar men, women, and children.

The Achuar people have an amazing success story, and they have asked our speaker to share it with you. That is the subject of his talk this morning: **David & Goliath in the Amazon: How a Small Indigenous Group Triumphed over Big Oil**

Please welcome Larry Lansburgh.

Note that the introduction avoids generalizations and gives specific details about my qualifications.

Once, I asked a friend introduce me, but I made the mistake of not providing an introduction. He went on and on about what a wonderful guy I was. Waiting backstage, I could feel the energy drain out of the audience. They weren't there because of my charm or my sterling character. They had come because they wanted to hear someone who was qualified to speak about Amazonian indigenous people.

My presentation never recovered. There was just no juice in the audience, and it wasn't their fault. It was mine. By not furnishing a strong introduction, I had ignored their reason for attending.

As bad as this introduction was, I heard one that was worse.

The worst introduction I have ever heard

During a trip to Seattle, I attended a presentation given by a physician who was promoting her new book about prenatal care. I already knew she was strongly qualified to speak. She went to great schools, and did her residency and years of clinical work in some of the country's finest hospitals. She had won awards for previous books.

But her presentation began badly because of the man who introduced her.

This guy blathered on and on about almost everything except the speaker's expertise. He even plugged his own book!

She was actually a very good speaker, but as the planner of her own presentation, she missed the mark. She should have written her own introduction and had someone else (someone trustworthy) to deliver it.

Your first words

When you walk out on stage (or to the front of the room), you have thirty seconds either to engage your audience or to lose them. You have no more time than that.

Should you begin with a joke?

No. A joke will almost certainly not address your audience's reasons for coming to your event. For a presentation I gave in Illinois, I considered opening with a joke about their governor at the time, Rod Blagojevich, who was under indictment for trying to sell Barak Obama's newly vacant U.S. Senate seat to the highest bidder. However, in spite of the temptation to get a laugh, I regained my sanity and decided not to begin with words that had nothing to do with my presentation.

The good news is that you don't need jokes, fancy graphics, or loud music to engage your audience. No matter the size of your audience, you simply need to connect with people on a personal level. You do this by being faithful to your "My Audience" worksheet.

You address their reasons for attending. You tell them how you can serve them.

Remember that all of them will be silently asking, "What's in this for me?"

Tell them. That is a strong opening.

Here are my first words in the keynote address at Cal Poly:

> My commitment to you this morning is to provide something of practical value, something you can use in your efforts toward a more sustainable human presence on planet earth.
> *(I immediately establish a relationship with the audience—my commitment to them—and I address their reasons for attending.)*

> Many aspects of sustainability deserve our passion and our actions, but this morning, I'll concentrate on one area—how a small indigenous group triumphed over big oil.
> *(I provide a quick summary.)*

They beat Big Oil with tactics that are sophisticated, ethical, and effective. For almost twenty years now, the Achuar people have used those tactics to protect their traditional way of life from corporations that would cheerfully destroy them and their pristine forest for short-term profit.

(By saying "Big Oil," I allude to the David and Goliath theme. Also, the summary becomes more detailed, and promises to reveal some powerful tactics.)

Achuar men and women have told me they want to share their experiences_with you. I'm convinced people everywhere—and each of you—can use Achuar tactics to change conditions that are harmful and unsustainable.

(Again, I'm connecting with my audience and reassuring them that I'm going to provide something they can really use.)

To write or not to write your first words

Write. Those first thirty seconds are so important that I write my first words out, and I memorize them. I rehearse my opening more times than I can count.

If you do this, you will not sound stilted or mechanical to your audience. You will sound confident, articulate, self-assured. By the way, memorize your ending too. More about this in Chapter 5.

When I develop a new presentation, I write the entire thing out, and then rehearse with the text. I go over it again and again. I don't try to memorize the whole presentation, but after days of rehearsal, I'm very familiar with it. Then I turn the text into an outline, which I use during the presentation to make sure I stay on track.

Write and rehearse. If you just wing it, your presentation won't fly.

Very poor first words

Once I attended a presentation about indigenous people in Indonesia, and how logging is destroying their culture. The speaker's first words went something like this:

> Uh... first I'd like to thank Sam Smith for ... uh... setting up the overhead projector, and... uh... the good folks here at the Veterans' Hall, and uh....

This speaker clearly communicated that he was about to bore us out of our skulls, and over the next hour and a half, he did exactly that. He had thirty seconds either to engage us or to lose us. He immediately lost us because he failed to establish a relationship with us. He turned away from his audience and instead established his relationship with Sam Smith and the good folks at the Veterans' Hall.

Sam Smith and the good folks at the Veterans' Hall made it possible for this speaker's event to take place, so thanks were definitely in order. But the speaker should have thanked them later.

A great beginning always focuses on the audience.

It's good manners to briefly thank the person who introduced you ("Thank you, Jan."), but then use those critical first thirty seconds to establish an authentic rapport with your audience.

By the way, at the end of the painful presentation about logging in Indonesia, I estimated that the speaker had probably said "uh" five hundred times. Once or twice is no big deal, but five hundred was extremely distracting. Although I'm convinced you don't have to be a great speaker to give a great presentation, why not be a terrific speaker giving a stellar presentation? In Chapter 7, you can find out how to be a terrific speaker.

That awful presentation failed in another way. It went on far too long.

The next chapter shows you how to design the main body of your presentation—how to keep your great opening and your great ending close together.

CHAPTER 4

Keep Them Close Together

If you ask a group of people to raise their hands if they have ever seen a friend's slide show, almost everyone will raise a hand. After the hands go down, ask the group to raise their hands again if they thought their friend's slideshow was too long. All of the same hands will go into the air again.

Several years ago, my wife and I went to a friend's house for a slideshow. It went on so long that my wife actually stood up and told our host to stop.

> ***I'll be brief.***
> Usually the first words uttered by a long-winded, boring speaker.

Never say you'll be brief. Just <u>be</u> brief.

The purpose of your presentation is to inform, entertain, inspire, or invite. Or any combination of these. No matter what your purpose, no matter how good a speaker you are, if your presentation is too long, you will bore your audience. You might have done everything right at first and had a fantastic opening. But if you go on too long, your audience will be bored, and you will have broken your bond with them. You will not have informed, entertained, inspired, or invited effectively.

Rehearsal is the most effective way to keep the beginning close to the ending.

Rehearsal

There is an old joke about a guy from the Midwest who was in New York to attend a concert in Carnegie Hall. But the Midwesterner got lost. He spotted a fellow on the street and asked, "How do I get to Carnegie Hall?"

The fellow answered, "Practice, practice, practice."

> *If you want to be good, you have to practice, practice, practice.*
> Ray Bradbury (1920 - 2012)
> Author

That is your key: Practice. You have already determined how long your presentation will be. Now practice with a stopwatch. The first two or three times you rehearse, your stopwatch will tell you your presentation is too long. The sinking feeling you have in your stomach is actually a good thing. It's an indication that you have the chance to avoid giving a long, and therefore boring, presentation.

Never, ever bore your audience.

An agonizing way to keep your beginning and your ending close together

Be willing to leave some material out, even if you love it. It's easy to delete things that are clearly irrelevant. But you may have to let go of some good stuff too, and that's always painful.

Let's say you're representing an environmental organization, and the purpose of your presentation is to invite people to help clean up a stretch of the local river. You've taken lots of powerful before-and-after photos of last year's cleanup. Do you really need to show all twenty-five if your stopwatch tells you you're running long? How about three photos? If you're still running long, how about one?

Let's say you're planning to have five people come up on the stage and give testimonials about how rewarding it was for them to participate in the river cleanup. In rehearsal, they all do a great job. But the stopwatch tells you the event is running long. It will be tough, but tell two of them that there's not enough time to use them. Their feelings are important, but your relationship with your audience is more important.

It's fantastic, but does it help your presentation?

During the production of my documentary film about the Achuar people, *Dream People of the Amazon*, I filmed an indigenous people's protest march through the streets of Quito, the capital of Ecuador. The march ended unexpectedly when we came up against a solid wall of police, all dressed in their riot gear, all carrying billy clubs, all backed up by troops ready to use tear gas. Some of the indigenous marchers came right up to the policemen's shields, and began chanting and gesturing with their spears.

I decided that, in spite of the risk, I should put myself and my camera between the line of riot police and the spear-carrying marchers. I got a spectacular shot.

But I left it out of the film.

Oh, I was powerfully tempted to leave it in. I had taken a risk to get it. The composition and camera moves were excellent. I loved the shot then, and I still do.

But if I had kept it in, I would have had to stop and explain that the indigenous men's seemingly aggressive gestures with their spears were really their way of saying, "We're warriors like you, but we come in peace." Some things just don't translate between different cultures without a lot of explanation, and the shot would have interrupted the flow of the film. I'm glad I left it out.

Another way to keep your great beginning and your great ending close together is to avoid losing track of time.

> *If I had more time, I would have written you a shorter letter.*
> Blaise Pascal (1623 - 1662)
> Philosopher

The elastic nature of time

In planning your presentation, you've rigorously left out non-essential elements. You've made sure you're not wandering off the subject. You've rehearsed with a stopwatch. The person introducing you has established your expertise. With your first words, you have established an authentic rapport with your audience.

But one more trap, one more brain-fade, can still spoil your presentation.

You <u>will</u> lose track of time. All of us speakers lose track of time when we're on stage or at the front of the room.

The way around this is to ask someone to be your timekeeper. Have that person sit in the front row, or anywhere he or she is clearly visible to you, and signal when your time is up.

I advised a client to do this, and he replied he didn't need a timekeeper because he could easily see the big clock on the back wall of the room. I said that when he was up in front of his audience, the big clock would become invisible. It did, and his presentation ran too long.

You might be tempted just to glance at your wristwatch. But it's poor body language because it's distracting for your audience. If you must use it, take it off and put it on the lectern. Or put a stopwatch on the lectern. Just remember that either one of those timepieces will probably become just as invisible as the big clock on the wall.

Use a timekeeper.

> *Always leave your audience wanting more.*
> Larry Lansburgh, Sr.

A friend of mine was in charge of a presentation, but she was not the speaker. The speaker was a well-known expert in his field. My friend told the speaker that she would act as a timekeeper. But the man said he would know when to stop. (After all, he was an expert.) Like many experts, he mistakenly believed his brilliance would guarantee an excellent presentation. He rambled on and on, and the presentation went far too long. My friend sat in agony while she watched the audience squirm with boredom. They definitely did not want more.

Other crucial techniques for a stellar presentation

Your middle section has to keep your beginning close to your ending, but you also have other essential tasks. You need to:
- Check equipment

- Help people remember what you say
- Avoid PowerPoint abuse
- Thank people
- Decide whether or not to use notes

Check equipment

Several years ago, I attended a presentation plagued by equipment problems. They wanted to show a short video, but after the audience sat down, they were still looking for the cable that attached the DVD player to the projector. When they couldn't find the cable, they put the DVD into a laptop. Then everybody had to huddle around the computer, but only two or three people could see the image clearly.

The solution is simplicity itself. At least an hour before showtime, make sure the equipment is working flawlessly. If it's not, you'll probably have enough time to fix things.

Help people remember what you say

Clearly, it's essential that people in your audience remember what you say. Stories are a powerful tool. This book is filled with stories. I will end this chapter with a story.

> *There's always room for a story that can transport people to another place.*
> J.K. Rowling (1965 -)
> Author

When I speak about the tactics the Achuar people use to keep the oil companies out of their territory, I don't just list the tactics and speak in generalities. I illustrate each tactic with a true story.

Here's a story I love. One day in a remote settlement in the Amazon rain forest, I was in a typical Achuar house. It had a thatched roof, posts with no walls, and a dirt floor. In the middle of the floor was a permanent cooking fire. A little girl, four or five years old, was playing next to the fire, just a foot or so from the flames. And she was playing with a full-size, razor-sharp machete. Not a single adult showed the slightest concern. The Achuar people love their children and are always kind to them, but from a very early age, Achuar children are expected to be responsible for their own safety and to be competent in the world of the rain forest.

Fostering competence in children is an Achuar tactic because the threat of oil operations will probably go on for generations. Some of those kids need to be competent in dealing not only with the rain forest, but also with threats from the outside world. Consequently, the Achuar community fosters children's competence in one of the languages of that world, a language totally unrelated to Achuar—Spanish, the national language of Ecuador. Today most Achuar kids are effortlessly bilingual.

People's mental image of the little girl playing next to the fire with the machete vividly anchors the concept of competence in children.

Avoid PowerPoint abuse

Consider not using it at all. Steve Jobs famously said, "People who know what they're talking about don't need PowerPoint."

PowerPoint can make presenters sloppy, make them think they don't have to master their subject. Some presenters think they can just use the technology to shine a bunch of information onto a screen, and they're off the hook as speakers. This is a recipe for a bad presentation.

To me, PowerPoint is like a chainsaw. Use a chainsaw badly, and you get hurt. Use it well, and you get firewood. Used well, PowerPoint can help your audience visualize, and therefore remember what you say. To avoid PowerPoint abuse:

- Keep text very simple. Just use it to summarize.
- Avoid the "Triple Read." Don't read the slide to your audience while they have the same text on a handout.
- Use handouts for more detailed text.
- If photos or video will help people remember, use them, but do so sparingly.

- When you're done with a slide, go to a black slide. If you're speaking while there is a slide on the screen, your audience's attention will go to the screen and away from you.
- Don't use fancy transitions between slides, such as flips, page turns, and 3-dimensional spinning cubes. If you think you need this stuff to keep your audience's interest, then <u>you're</u> the one who needs to be more interesting.

Thank people

The middle portion of your presentation is the time to thank the people whose help was essential to your event. Find a place in the flow that is ideal for thanks. Don't thank them at the very end, because the end is an especially crucial point in your relationship with your audience. The next chapter will tell you how to have a great ending.

Decide whether or not to use notes

Use notes if you need to. Just know that notes are not a substitute for rehearsal. Once I saw someone speak entirely from his notes. But his delivery was halting and he had a lot of long pauses while he navigated his way through the material. Those pauses alone must have added ten or fifteen minutes to his presentation. It was clear he had not rehearsed enough, that he was using the notes as a crutch. It was a rubber crutch, and it let him down. It let his audience down too.

> *I've always considered myself to be just average talent and what I have is a ridiculous insane obsessiveness for practice and preparation.*
> Will Smith (1968 -)
> Actor

One more reason to keep your beginning close to your ending

During the American Civil War, in July of 1863, Union and Confederate forces slaughtered each other in the Battle of Gettysburg. After three days of fighting, thousands of soldiers lay dead on the battlefield.

The following November, with the war still raging in other parts of the country, civilians, military bands, and dignitaries gathered on the now-quiet battlefield at Gettysburg to commemorate the dead. One of the dignitaries was President Abraham Lincoln, who delivered one of the greatest speeches in the English language, his Gettysburg Address.

But another speaker gave an address before Lincoln spoke. Do you know who the other speaker was? Can you quote even three words from what he said? You're not alone. No one remembers him.

The other speaker was a renowned orator whose speech lasted two hours. Lincoln's Gettysburg Address lasted just over two minutes.

Ever since that day, no one has ever been criticized for giving a speech that was too short.

CHAPTER 5

Have a great ending

Many presenters don't have a clue how to finish, so this is where they seriously mess up. When it's time to bring things to a close, they don't actually say, "Gosh, what am I going to do now?" But you know that's exactly what they're thinking because they're wearing a confused "deer in the headlights" expression. I watched one presenter get the stricken look on his face, and then he actually asked his audience, "Should I keep going?"

No one said, "Yes." And no one said what everyone was probably thinking: "No. Don't keep going. Someone get the hook." This left the audience and the presenter in a state of confusion. Confusion is deeply unsatisfying.

To avoid end-of-the-event confusion, don't ask your audience how and when you should end. It's up to you.

And you <u>will</u> create a great ending. Unlike many other presenters, you will not mess up.

You have done brilliantly so far. You engaged and enrolled your audience with a beginning that speaks directly to them and their reasons for coming to your presentation. You established and maintained a genuine rapport with them.

You delivered the essentials of your presentation with a middle section tightly focused on the subject matter. Your judicious use of slides and videos perfectly illustrated the essence of your presentation. Your projection equipment worked perfectly. Your stories will help people remember what you said. Your use of PowerPoint was sparing, and therefore effective. You rehearsed with a stopwatch, so your presentation hasn't run too long.

Now your timekeeper signals you that it's time to bring the presentation to a close.

Where other presenters might get it wrong, you get it right. You know the anatomy of a great ending.

What constitutes a great ending?

A great ending is clear and definite. It's as simple as that.

Don't ramble on. Just communicate clearly that you're finished, accept the applause, and walk offstage.

> *Begin at the beginning and go on till you come to the end: then stop.*
> Lewis Carroll (1832 - 1898)
> Author

In Chapter 3, I stress the importance of writing and memorizing a great opening. It's the same with the ending. For example, if you want to end with a quotation, memorize it. If you're going to end with a summary, write it and memorize it.

Here are the steps in a great ending:

1. Summarize.

Once again, answer the audience's primary question, "What's in it for me?" For example, "The Achuar people are using highly effective tactics to defend their way of life. You can begin using those same tactics today. They are ...."

As part of your summary, you might add something new and surprising, but relevant to your theme. By the time I'm ready to end my presentation about the Achuar and their struggle to defend their territory from the oil companies, my audience knows oil operations would mean the literal extinction of this community. Sometimes I finish by saying that all the oil under Achuar territory would satisfy the petroleum needs of the United States for only twenty-one days. Every time I say this, the audience gasps.

Another possibility is to end with a relevant quotation. I finished my presentation to the California Students Sustainability Convergence by acknowledging my audience for making the world a better place.

I ended with the famous words of anthropologist Margaret Mead: "Never doubt that a small group of thoughtful, committed citizens can change the world. Indeed, it is the only thing that ever has."

2. Say, "Thank you."

    Your audience will recognize "thank you" as a clear and definite ending, and they will applaud.

3. Accept your audience's applause.

    The applause isn't truly the end because you are still in relationship with them while they are clapping. So don't exit quite yet. Accept the applause. Let it in. Enjoy it!

4. Leave.

    The time to leave the stage or move to the side of the room is when the applause begins to die down.

> *Great is the art of beginning, but greater the art is of ending.*
> Henry Wadsworth Longfellow (1807 - 1882)
> Poet and educator

Three of the worst endings I have ever witnessed

One speaker said, "Uh, well, I guess I've run out of time."

(Of course you've run out of time. You obviously didn't rehearse with a stopwatch. You should have said, "Thank you for coming. If you have questions, I'll be available." You should have then accepted the applause and walked to another part of the room to speak with people who wanted to stick around.)

In a recital in someone's home, a guy played the guitar and sang songs he had written. Toward the end, he said, "You wanna hear more?"

(No! You've been on far too long. End the recital by saying, "For my final piece, I'll play-." When you finish that piece, accept the applause and leave. If your audience wants to hear more, their applause will tell you they want an encore.)

In one presentation, the host showed a documentary film. After the film, he picked up the microphone and started talking again—while the audience was walking out.

(Hey! The audience knows your presentation is over, but obviously you don't. Before the movie began, you should have encouraged the audience to visit the various organizations' tables around the room after the movie. When the movie ends, that's the end of the presentation, so stay away from the microphone.)

Questions and answers

A question-and-answer period may be appropriate. It's up to you. Here are the keys to a successful question-and-answer period:

If you're speaking in a large space, repeat the question. It's possible that not everyone in your audience has heard the question.

Don't say, "Good question." If you do, you will seem to be implying that other people's questions are not so good.

Remember you have an ally sitting in the front row—your timekeeper, who has been watching the clock so you don't have to. Now he or she silently signals you your time is up. Whatever you do, don't say something like "Well, my timekeeper tells me I've run out of time." That's lame because it breaks your relationship with your audience. The audience should never be aware of your timekeeper. When you see your timekeeper's signal:

1. Ask for one more question, and answer it. Even if there are still people eager to ask questions (lots of hands in the air), you need to have a clear, crisp ending.
2. Say you'll be available for informal conversations.
3. As before, summarize, or end with something new and surprising, or use a good quotation.
4. Say "Thank you."
5. Accept the applause.
6. Walk off the stage.

> *Get on stage, get off,
> and leave 'em applauding.*
> Larry Lansburgh, Sr.

Be available after your presentation.

The informal conversations after my presentations are always deeply rewarding. My audience is no longer a large group of people, but now individuals with whom I can have a conversation. I get to be face to face with people who have paid me the honor of coming to my presentation.

Stick around. Be one of the last people to leave the room.

CHAPTER 6

The Invitational Presentation

In this type of presentation, you're going to invite your audience to do something.

If you're a financial advisor giving an investment seminar, you might invite people to become clients. If you're the director of volunteers at a local convalescent hospital, you might invite a group of high school students to become volunteers. Later in this chapter, you'll see sample worksheets for these presentations.

It is definitely an invitation. Some will accept, and some will not. Those audience members who accept will do so because they will have found your invitation irresistible—for the very good reason that you will offer a genuine benefit along with your invitation.

I almost labeled this a "persuasive presentation," but this sets the wrong tone. It's not about sales techniques, or talking people into doing things. I'm just not a hard-sell kind of person, so if you're looking for hard-sell techniques, I'm sure there are plenty of other books you could consult.

In doing my research on other people's presentations, I attended one that was pure hard-sell. It was put on by a company selling herbal health products through multi-level marketing (MLM). There's nothing wrong with MLM when it's coupled with ethical business practices. There's nothing wrong with an honest attempt to sell something, and many people are convinced that herbal remedies work well. But this presentation was clearly deceptive.

One of the first things the speaker mentioned was that he was not allowed to say one of his products could cure cancer. Throughout the evening he kept repeating, "This can't cure cancer. This can't cure cancer." Strictly speaking, he was telling the truth, but the implication was the opposite. He was implying his product could cure cancer, but he just wasn't allowed to say so.

He also said that joining his MLM downline was all about helping people. "Now, I make $20,000 a week," he mentioned casually.

Everyone in the audience leaned forward in their chairs. Even I leaned forward. Twenty thou a week sounded pretty good, even though I was just there as a researcher.

"But," he continued, "it's really not about the money. It's about helping people."

Nonsense. All business is about the money. And he never mentioned the fact that five percent of people in multi-level marketing make ninety-five percent of the money. Most or even all of the people who signed up with him would never make much money selling herbal remedies.

Yes, he was promising a benefit, but the promise was false (or at least partially true).

Your invitational presentation

Your presentation can be extremely effective, whether or not you're not a salesperson. All you need to do is create a presentation that is not "persuasive," but invitational. You can do so by coupling your invitation with a genuine benefit.

Planning your invitational presentation

Start with this worksheet. It's a slightly expanded version of the one in Chapter 3.

Invitational Presentation
My Audience

Who is my audience?

What are their reasons for attending?

What is the specific action I am inviting them to take?

If they do what I invite them to do, what is the benefit to them?

Are there additional ways I can serve my audience?

With all of the above in mind, what is a compelling title for the presentation?

How long will this presentation be?

Once you've answered these questions, your presentation should then follow the Simple Key to Great Presentations. But in this type of presentation, you're going to invite your audience to take a specific action. The action might be something they haven't ever considered. It might even be something they'll resist. But if you communicate a genuine, achievable benefit, you will have an effective presentation.

Sample worksheets

Worksheets for a financial advisor and the director of volunteers for a convalescent hospital might look like these.

FINANCIAL ADVISOR

Invitational Presentation
My Audience

Who is my audience?
Couples and singles within five years of retirement

What are their reasons for attending?
Most will be interested in their financial options during retirement. But some will just come for the free lunch.

What is the specific action I am inviting them to take?
Go to the back of the room and sign up as a client with Pat.

If they do what I invite them to do, what is the benefit to them?
They can begin the process of creating the financial flexibility and safety necessary for a stress-free retirement.

Are there additional ways I can serve my audience?
For those who sign up, I can help provide peace of mind, more available money during retirement (and

therefore more options such as travel and financial plans for the grandchildren), less stress and worry about money.

With all of the above in mind, what is a compelling title for the presentation?

Financial Strength and Peace of Mind When You Retire

How long will this presentation be?

Thirty minutes, plus ten to fifteen minutes of questions and answers. Total of forty to forty-five minutes.

DIRECTOR OF VOLUNTEERS FOR A CONVALESCENT HOSPITAL

Invitational Presentation
My Audience

Who is my audience?

Juniors and seniors in the local high school. I am especially trying to reach students who will be going to college. Anyone with plans to enter the health care field would be ideal.

What are their reasons for attending?

Their teachers have encouraged them to attend, but attendance is not mandatory. They might be interested in some kind of volunteer work that ties in with their desire to go into health care.

What is the specific action I am inviting them to take?

Become a volunteer at Elm Street Convalescent Hospital by going to the back of the room and signing up with either Ms. Greene or Ms. Kelley.

If they do what I invite them to do, what is the benefit to them?
They will have an extracurricular activity that could give them a competitive edge when they apply for college.

Are there additional ways I can serve my audience?
I can offer them an opportunity to expand their horizons and gain the satisfaction of being more active members of the community.

With all of the above in mind, what is a compelling title for the presentation?
Volunteering: The Fast Track to Your Future

How long will this presentation be?
I only have twenty minutes.

My invitational presentation in the Amazon rain forest

By far, the greatest threat to the Achuar way of life comes from oil companies, and I wanted to make a film that would bring this threat to the world's attention. It is easy to assault the environment and violate human rights if the only ones who know about it are the victims and the perpetrators. It becomes far more difficult if the world knows about it.

Clearly, I couldn't just assemble a film crew, march into the Amazon rain forest of southeastern Ecuador, and start pointing cameras at people. For one thing, the Achuar don't like cameras. How was I going to make a film about people who don't want their pictures taken? I'd face this issue later, if I got permission to make the film.

My first step was to ask permission from the president of the Achuar federation. He said the federation makes decisions by consensus, so I would have to ask the assembly of leaders when they got together for their annual congress. He asked me to come to Achuar territory and present my ideas to the group.

This called for a presentation—an invitational presentation.

My first step was to answer the questions on my worksheet, which is on the next page.

Invitational Presentation
My Audience

Who is my audience?

About 150 leaders of the Achuar people. They are the elected representatives of their people. There is no hereditary leadership in this culture. It is a pure meritocracy.

They know that oil lies under their territory, and the outside world would gladly poison their pristine forest and obliterate their way of life to get the oil.

Leaders here are tough, intelligent people, and they learn very quickly.

Their native language, Achuar, is related to no other language on earth, other than a few local varieties. But one-half to two-thirds of my audience understand Spanish, the national language of Ecuador. Fortunately, my Spanish is pretty good, so I'll use it for my presentation. An interpreter will then translate my Spanish to Achuar.

What are their reasons for attending the conference?

To discuss important issues, make group decisions, and take appropriate actions.

What is the specific action I am inviting them to take?
To give me permission to make a documentary film about them.

If they do what I invite them to do, what will be the benefit to them?
By bringing the Achuar struggle for survival to the world's attention, this film could be part of their defense against destruction by the industrialized world.

Are there additional ways I can serve my audience?
Once completed, the film could be part of live presentations that I would make. In effect, I would be one of the spokesmen for the Achuar people.

With all of the above in mind, what is a compelling title for the presentation?
In this case, no title. I'm just one of many speakers.

How long will this presentation be?
Probably five minutes at most.

My presentation begins

The congress was held in a typical rain forest building. It had a dirt floor and no walls. Posts held up the thatched roof. Delegates and visitors (including me) sat on rows of big logs. People addressing the delegates stood on a low wooden platform. Issues up for discussion included relations with the Ecuadorian government, ties with other indigenous groups, a particularly harmful shaman in one village, a small herd of newly introduced cattle that were beginning to destroy a few acres the rain forest, and the threat from an oil company that wanted to drill in Achuar territory.

My introduction

In Chapter 3, I advise you to create your own introduction for someone else to deliver. It's sound advice, but this time I decided to ignore it. The president of the federation said he would introduce me. Because I would be speaking to people of a very different culture, I felt sure his words would resonate far better with the audience than anything I could create. His introduction was in Achuar, so I didn't understand a word he said. But he was brief, and it must have been a good introduction because, as I stepped onto the speaker's platform, I had my audience's full attention.

My first words

Also in Chapter 3, I urge you to craft your first words very carefully. I definitely followed this advice. I felt that, in spite of immense cultural differences, I still had about thirty seconds to authentically connect with my audience. Speaking of differences, as I stood there, I was aware I didn't look at all like most of the people sitting on the logs. Amazonian indigenous people have straight black hair, brown eyes, beautiful brown-gold complexions, and a tall man is about five-seven. I am six feet tall, brown hair, blue eyes, and a light complexion.

Every man in my audience wore a feathered head-dress and a stern expression. Every man's face was covered with designs made with the red juice of the achiote berry. Not a soul spoke English.

Very few outsiders speak Achuar well. No North Americans speak more than a few phrases in Achuar. As a sign of my respect, for the first thirty seconds I spoke in Achuar, the audience's own language.

The stern expressions on the warriors' faces turned to smiles, and everyone applauded.

Several days earlier, I had asked a young Spanish-speaking Achuar man to help me with those first words. I didn't ask him to translate my Spanish, but rather to tell me what would be appropriate words for an Achuar audience. He spoke the Achuar words, I wrote them down as best I could, and he told me the meaning in Spanish. Through brute force repetition, I committed those thirty seconds of Achuar to memory.

The invitation

My presentation to the leaders of the Achuar people involved absolutely no "salesmanship," and I did not invent some theoretical benefit. Having switched from my extremely limited Achuar to my adequate Spanish, I said a film could be a way for more people in the outside world to learn about the Achuar defense of their homeland. Then I asked if they thought such a film would serve them. If so, I would make it happen. Considering their aversion to being photographed, I said if they did not want a film, I would understand. I thanked them for their consideration, and left the platform.

The debate immediately began—in their native language, of course—so I had no idea what the leaders were saying. After about ten minutes, I learned they had approved the project. They would check with several villages, and my small film crew and I would only go into those villages where the people would tolerate our cameras.

Your invitational presentation

Yes, you want your audience to buy your new software, or sign up for your relationship seminar, or be part of your two-week yoga class in Hawaii. But you are not going to persuade them to do anything. You are going to invite them.

There is a difference.

Some people in your audience may refuse your invitation. Those who accept will do so because they find the benefit irresistible.

Start with the worksheet in this chapter. You can download it free from my web site (www.AmazonSpeaker.com).

Everyone in your audience will be asking themselves, "What's in this for me?" Remember what you wrote in your worksheet and tell them.

And, of course, your invitational presentation needs to follow the Simple Key to Great Presentations:

**Have a great beginning.
Have a great ending.
Keep them close together.**

Features *versus* benefits

In an invitational presentation, benefits are far more powerful than features. Steve Jobs understood this.

Imagine yourself in the audience back in 2001, when Jobs introduced the first iPod. Think how you would have reacted if he had said, "The iPod has a 5 GB hard drive with a 160 Kbps MP3 format, a high output amplifier of 60 mW, a FireWire port, a standard 3.5-mm headphone jack in a white and stainless steel case, a 2-inch white backlit LCD display, and a battery life of ten hours."

You would have fallen asleep before he got to the high output amplifier of 60 mW.

In fact, Jobs said little or nothing about features.

Instead, he simply said, "This amazing little device holds a thousand songs. And it goes right in my pocket."

You can see this part of Jobs' presentation on YouTube: (http://www.youtube.com/watch?v=6SUJNspeux8)

Whether you're inviting your audience to get screened for high blood pressure, or inviting them to buy something from you, communicate benefits and have a clear call to action.

In the 1920's, very few people in the rural Midwest had telephones. A story has it that two rival salesmen were working in the same area, going door-to-door trying to sell phone service. One salesman brilliantly described the new technology. In great detail, he told how the diaphragm in the mouthpiece vibrated as a person spoke, changing acoustic energy into a fluctuating electrical current by means of an electrode. He spoke eloquently about volts, amps, ohms, and specific gauges of wire. This man sold no telephones, and quit his job in despair.

The other salesman simply said, "If you have a telephone, you can talk to your neighbors without ever leaving the house. Would you like to buy a telephone now?"

He got rich from his commissions.

CHAPTER 7

Final Thoughts

You can be a mediocre speaker and still deliver an excellent presentation if you have a great beginning, a great ending, and you keep them close together.

Also, if you do nothing more than avoid the mistakes you've read about in this book, you will deliver a much better presentation than most other people. The presentation on logging in Indonesia would have been far better if the speaker hadn't said "uh" in almost every sentence. One of the differences between a good speaker and a poor one is that the good speaker simply does fewer things that are distracting or annoying.

Speaking of distracting and annoying, many years ago I gave a short talk that a friend videotaped. My friend told me to take the videocassette home and watch it. I did so, and I was horrified.

My hand gestures were absolutely embarrassing. I looked like an orchestra conductor on speed batting away swarms of angry bees. I had no idea that my body language was so distracting. My feelings of pain and embarrassment were no fun, but they made me want to be a better speaker.

I urge you to become a better speaker, but it won't happen by reading a book, including this one. Speaking is like playing a musical instrument, or doing carpentry, or landing an airplane. You can read about it all you want. Doing it is the only way to get good.

You can become a good speaker, or even a great one, by joining Toastmasters International.

Toastmasters

The Toastmasters website (Toastmasters.org) will help you find a club near you. On the home page, click on the "Find a location near you" button. Follow the prompts and you'll find the contact information to get you started.

You'll quickly discover that the members of your local Toastmasters club are warm, welcoming, and very supportive. With patience and kindness, members evaluate one another's presentations, and this really helps to hone speaking skills. In my Toastmasters club, I've seen people start as quivering lumps of terror and incompetence. In just a few months, they had become confident and riveting speakers.

Toastmasters is both effective and economical.

Now, imagine what you can accomplish if you're not only a wonderful speaker, but you also use the Simple Key to Great Presentations to structure an event that could change someone's life.

A life-changing presentation

In San Francisco, California in the early 1990's, I went to a presentation that changed the course of my life.

I came to the presentation unsure of what to expect. I knew the gathering was an introduction to a new non-profit organization that was somehow in partnership with a small group of indigenous people in the Amazon rain forest. This sounded interesting. I also knew the organization wanted to enroll new members. Understandable, but I've never been much of a joiner, so my defenses were up.

When the presentation was over, something had convinced me that this organization not only had passionate, committed people, but also was extremely well run. I wrote a check and became a proud new member.

What was it about the presentation that so quickly enrolled me? The organization's purpose was commendable—to help the group of Amazonian indigenous people defend themselves from destruction by oil operations—but the world has plenty of good causes. Certainly the speakers were passionate and articulate, but something else had enrolled me.

It was the event's structure. It had a great beginning, a great ending, and those two elements were close together. It followed the Simple Key to Great

Presentations, which gave me confidence in the organization.

The event began on time. It was focused not just on the indigenous people, but also on us, the audience. They showed some slides, but no one was fumbling around at the last minute trying to make the equipment work; they had obviously tested it long before we arrived. And the presentation ended precisely when they said it was going to end, which convinced me these were people who keep their word. The whole event was crisp.

The organization is called The Pachamama Alliance (www.pachamama.org). A non-profit with headquarters in San Francisco, California, it is in partnership with the Achuar people, whom you have read about in this book. Several times a year, Pachamama organizes trips for small groups to go into Achuar territory. And what a territory it is—two million acres of unspoiled, primeval rain forest, one of the most biologically diverse areas on earth. I went on one of those trips. Then I led a trip, in partnership with one of Pachamama's Ecuadorian colleagues. After that, I made a documentary film, *Dream*

People of the Amazon, which reveals the tactics the Achuar people are using so successfully in their defense of their rain forest home. Once the film was finished, I began to give presentations about the Achuar for audiences all over the US.

That one presentation by the Pachamama Alliance led to adventures in the Amazon rain forest and deeply satisfying work as a speaker.

> *Hi Larry,*
> *Thank you for sharing with us your Amazon documentary and your experiences in making it. We still talk about your visit here. You've even inspired one of my classmates to do a research paper based on your presentation.*
> Julie Provenza
> Class of 2011, Elmhurst College
> Elmhurst, Illinois

> *As a member of the audience, I loved your presentation, your documentary, and the sense of hope that engulfed us all. Michigan Tech and the town of Houghton were so fortunate to have you. I only hope you can make it back up here to see us again sometime. Thank you.*
> Cathy Campbell-Olszewski
> Houghton, Michigan

I'll never know how many of my audience members have been inspired by the success story of the Achuar people. I'll never know about the people they have inspired in turn. But I do know the Simple Key to Great Presentations is the foundation of my relationship with my audiences. I could not have inspired, or even entertained, anyone with a presentation people found boring, annoying, unfocused, and far too long.

Larry Lansburgh's thought provoking presentation on the triumphs of the Achuar people of Ecuador in preserving their land and their culture mesmerized our audience on many different levels.
Beverly Sanford, Ph.D.
Executive Director & CEO
SciWorks Science Center and Environmental Park
Winston-Salem, North Carolina

Your presentations

If you need to invite people to take an action, if you need to inspire, entertain, or inform them, the Simple Key to Great Presentations will amplify your voice. Your voice could very well change lives.

Whatever you do, or dream you can, begin it. Boldness has genius and power and magic in it.
Johann Wolfgang von Goethe (1749 - 1832)
Writer, poet, and politician

May the Simple Key to Great Presentations serve you well.

Has this book helped you? If so, please visit my web site and give me your comments.

Coaching and Consultation for Your Presentations

www.AmazonSpeaker.com

Acknowledgements

My mother, Janet Lansburgh (1911 - 1972), was a writer. She told me the best way to write is to apply the seat of your pants to a chair for long periods of time. But even if you do, she continued, you can't write a book all by yourself.

I haven't written *The Simple Key to Great Presentations* all by myself.

My wife, Sarah, has a constant and unstoppable enthusiasm for all my projects. While I was writing, she always encouraged me to apply the seat of my pants to my chair, especially when I didn't want to. She was incredibly supportive every time I left home for the Amazon rain forest.

Some extraordinary people took on the task of reading and commenting on my early drafts. My deep gratitude goes to Peter Van Zant, Patt Lind-Kyle, David Kyle, Fritz Kasten, Sarah Harper-Lansburgh, Susan Greene, Val Jon Farris, and Georgia Dow.

If I had tried to get the Academy Award nomination all by myself, there would not have been one. My brother, Brian Lansburgh, was my partner in the film. He knows how to put on a show—on the screen, in person, and in print. Brian's comments while I was writing were extremely valuable.

As Brian and I grew up, our father, Larry Lansburgh (1911 - 2001) instilled in us the gems of showmanship that run through these pages. With two Academy Awards to his name, he knew what he was talking about.

Finally, I truly appreciate all the people whose presentations I have attended. Some of those people followed the Simple Key to Great Presentations. Some did not. But by stepping in front of an audience and speaking, they all contributed mightily to this book.

The Author

Larry Lansburgh is an Academy Award-nominated and Emmy-winning documentary filmmaker. As an experienced public speaker, he also coaches and consults organizations and individuals who need to improve their presentations.

Over the years, he has created hundreds of presentations, on film and video as well as live events. Many times, he has been the sole speaker. On other occasions, he did not speak at all, but as the director was responsible for the event's success.

Larry's background includes work as a partner and chief copywriter in an advertising agency, and five years teaching business writing courses at the University of California Santa Cruz Extension.

Coaching and Consultation for Your Presentations
www.AmazonSpeaker.com

Made in the USA
Middletown, DE
11 February 2015